Imaginary Gardens

Imaginary Gardens

Billy Mills

hardPressed poetry

Published by hardPressed poetry

http://hardpressedpoetry.blogspot.com/
hardpressedpoetry@gmail.com

Copyright © Billy Mills 2012

Cover photograph copyright © Catherine Walsh 2012
Cover design by hardPressed poetry with Maurice O'Connor

ISBN: 978-1-872781-04-4

All rights reserved.
No part of this publication may be reproduced in any form or by any means without prior permission of the publisher.

A few pages of this poem were published in Cleaves Journal Issue 2.

these trees
this grove
this garden

lost
in morning

the very edge
of day

an order
sun imposes
random

these shrubs
these beds
this pathway

stand & wonder
why these walls
these trees
that very foxglove

wait now
spring
will come
again

around the statue
the blue forget-me-nots

drift of lawn   trees
            wall behind
all gone now
under brick & tar

buried & lost
almost
but that these words
recall
nearing perfection
slowly

sit in the dark
& wait
in the light
& wait

as if one could
as if the day meant
something the sun
the waning light

this time spent utterly
this life itself
lost under drift

transmogrified

drift wash over
grass some trees   nothing
accurate

what is it anyway
what is

nothing false out over
water   stone
a certain symmetry

sweeps silent round
& round

the white figure
standing

snail trail
on the path

a snail itself
on the path

curve
in the sand

what life what sound
grows here

the snail knows
to be a snail

the garden knows
nothing it is
an order flowers here
balance always

moving always
an unknown
river

variation flows
in which
we have come home
in which
we have never left

a certain
singularity

form

each step a switch
each switch a path
blind selection

strings of code
waiting the moment
the moment for action

a set of messages
that fade

that fly

garden gone to seed

elder & thorn
an old tin bath
grown through

lost
in the lushness

a house
reintegrating
& robin
singing
out

evening:

birds descend
(nervous) to feed
perhaps watchful
lost in the task
young now growing

nothing renews here
each new thing new
cycle broken
silence palpable
rest here in

memory wait
impromptu song
beneath
the run of days

sweet permitted fruit
wet leaves
humus

a corner where
men pitch snails
into
a smouldering tree trunk
& joke

& this is no new thing

smoke from a glowing trunk
the men chuck snails in
a quiet corner

who lived before
a formal order
hidden
whose fruit the arc
thyme drew before
the rains came

turn the earth & leave it
& time flows over
tilth forms dig in
matter level & rake & sow
in time for care
& entropy

to sit here morning summer
quiet everyone sleeping & not
yet heat a book a table family
blackbirds hidden singing
intermittently

a large flock of starlings move
slowly across the new-mown grass
feeding on what they find
in memory   an old house now

here young blackbirds sing
in the great oak beyond
redolent in evening sun

a tool a place of exchange
an imperfect mechanism people decide
old man first to market
each year ferns fruit a surplus

utility only cannot make it happen
beauty: a system of growth
flocks green this evening rise

walk
this way
to the falls

sound
grows
as you close

& falls
an iris
almost

behind
an air
almost

cool grey summer
small sun   less heat
whiff of rain   breeze

dry still this moment
next
nothing between no
sounds no words no
pattern

*

as if this smell
were something else

......a tool
not an ethic:

old man walking
his greenhouse
luxuriant
nurtured

child playing
absorbed   silent

these things
images
outside
listen

there is
nothing
clear now

floating
spores
in warm air

fronds uncurl
slowly

world curved
within

under glass

the bee needs
the flower needs
the bee

the seed needs
sun   water
proper medium

the process needs
rhythm
needs time

as needs be
seen here

to need
& yet
deny

still
in the garden
beauty

the code
unfolds
in time

there are no flowers
no stones no
uncertainty   everywhere

      * * * * *

wrack on the tide flows
a garden: look slow the pull
of water weaving branches
float anchored here scale
shingle clinks drag

sand pulled through
this surge this
resistance

flows & runs
through now   ever

& so the days go
& the nights go
& the water goes
& is the same

still here
in the garden
quiet now

what does it do
that only grows

a living tree
oak it is

leaves piled random
the wind does

as night comes
sleep escaping
distant now

grass   trees   stones
a single iris
suddenly insignificant

mould rising
as night proceeds
kindness remains

this stain
spreads
outwards

no sense
wanting

growth

fertility

none of these

(dream now)
solitary figure
tending flowers

each
in its time

it's time

& what wonders
roots under
where time is

out of death
we grow
that which grows

& enter it
entire
& human

only words
cannot
each in its time

it's time
rain heavy
nothing happening

flows & falls

a small
soft thing

earth
palpitant
cold

& out there
swimming
air

what now
not now
a leaf

pages
an echo
found

yielding
oak alive
(blackbirds)

song and leaf
shimmering

is life
not words

rain & sun
& cloud
& rain again

an hour
or not

another

water flows
does not flow
waits

no words
this day

silent almost
night almost
sleep nears

still almost
flourishing
rain moves
inexorable

water fills
dominates
the only
element

flows

slow   slow

            night

      fade   sleep

            gather

which   is

            which

sleep now   soft now

      start   again

as if it were
constant variance

small leaves curled
under themselves
recoiling from light

rain relentless
unremitting

it enters
it penetrates
it brings those gifts
that rain brings

that what is done well
is never done

great heap built
over time material
trust it   recur
a thing not known
but never lost:
lets go

to no line follow
an order: form
a sense beyond which
having moved
towards concord

as lines on earth
unseen   walk them
gather them all
and bury them
against
the coming season

which is to say
it is not so

sounds smells tastes
the movement   out

sun in its measure
year as it turns

light in the window
calls
(whichever)
calls

runs between
fingers & fertility

light gone again

nothing heals
but sleep

& if it sleeps
allow it

the lure
of memory
leaves

stick
to tarmac
wind eases   builds
eases

remember
there is silence
& is
& sleep makes it
so

morning: a
quantity of light
fractured & dimmed

banked against
day comes
slowly comes

clarity forms
stands sharp
against

each other
expands &
shifts

to ask what it is
to answer
no

to await
morning fog
ice on the car

road gritted
a drift
of reason

no a tiny
garden willow
cypress

to ask
& answer
no

no loss but this
a round of
entropy

of life its absence
gone but here in
these words this

mind these hands
that write this
voice what

work there is
is to be done
right here

or not at all
while time
allows

words flow out
& down
the page flows

out & meets
obstruction
the world flows

out
& down

who went out
who ran there
who rode

in a tale
a story

who shifted state
for the record

who held on
who dreamt
who found

love
it must be

who saw
this thing
& this

growing
it must be
soon

grass
& weeds
& wet
as winter
falls

dark
& crisp
betimes
(remember)

the year
vanishes
as you
were here

a simple
cure

love
endures

as night
assures
sleep
maybe

may be

year declines
forms occasional
moments of light
discreet & visible
sweet alarms not
sensible but less
there regard this
flower browns & droops
as night ascends
accepting

        as do I

rain again
against the light
insensible

morning
swish of traffic
ideas lost

sleep never
dream never
rest less

again

words only adequate
tilth a riddle
shake it out

warm & moist
a scent
walk in air

time each instance
step &
gradual grow

remember the day we went there
cold it was   clear winter
& walked out along the narrow
spring it was   road & through
the gateway entrance it did
so many approached different &
equally approximate some days
mean more than others & for us
good reason

                or summer even
hot & high meadows great clouds
of coloured wings they rose as
we walked through them humid
moments of clarity a village
dolls' houses they were almost pots
geraniums brilliant red on sills
balconies maybe even a bridge
but it was real it was on the map
& so we turned back

lizards
falling
still

flitting
clear &
live

each
in
place

wake
to see
the thingness of things

words stretch light
falls silent
over these

moments of wonder
sheer materiality
a world unmade
made one

that what is
is all there is
enough   & more

& all is lost
unless
you look

sleep now
under stars
a pattern
lacking meaning

which is not
we see it so
& know
nothing other

than this: it is
night draws in
this sky
attends

a road

wide
in places
not
in places

straight

a chord
clashes
without

three &
three
green these

notes
run   fall
run again

glisten
ice on
a song

listen: do not
sing it is
enough

ice rises
forms
this air

tattered leaves
thin branches
twigs rather

iced air
enters all
this is

not ending
air
again

big it was
& fertile
& well-tended

neat &
organised
& calming

& I was
small
& silent

finding
myself
alone

the kettle
on

sit
in the shade
& listen

world
turns
a sound

packets
of light
fall

hard
& gently
rain

crossing college green again
in memory weave a life so many
times the same thing: meaning
rhythm cars buses drifts
of people city lost now except
it is not & can never be

home of sorts left behind now
this conjunction cross between grey
piles & open spaces absorbed in time
the sting of marram on bare legs
bent under holding a stream
these dunes beyond recall

summer it must have been pleasing
to go roots hold it all now long gone
child playing aimlessly traffic
maps that which is all required
to move out from this centre (remember)
to find oneself climbing through

trees a certain animal presence
lift it now the flow of time
slows (remember) not occasions
a pattern feet made tracing
years returning to certain landfall
this motion constant silent among

unremembered lost now gone now except
here past gate & round the wall curves
follow a line   meet yourself
as once hazarded to leave others rushed
to meet language merely tends
these things it cannot comprehend

& cross the bridge
in relative stillness

in rain perhaps
sun perhaps

westward   look
the city reaches

domes curve beyond:
move on

if there is nothing
what is there

that which asks
that which is asked of

& if there is

rain on grass a sheen
fine lines luminous grey
the sky is certain
we set out

to where it was
we would arrive

steadily the air
clarifies light
the hills close in
(the usual ones)

& we are near again
the open door
eludes us
slips beyond
edge of vision

(not quite)

between rock
& rock
walking

small fields
grass sparse
in fissures
corners

ocean   below
wind   above

low walls promise
little & much

the great wall
looms & curves

grey   blue   grey

not timeless
but outside time

not sea
not mountain:
what lies between

call it
it comes
& is

longships moored
wooden streets

homes & workshops
lives entwined

haven perhaps
exchange even
a place to live

call it
& it is

some land
four fields say

predates us
outlives us

& so
begins

to flow
to form
to move beneath
the hand

& is not wealth
but a way
of going

words cannot tell
this range
of browns & greens
innumerable greys
but it is light
& water
& rock undiminished

as Omey is
sand
& wind
& walking

water cold
& necessary
to arrive
& then turn back
& see what it is

alive

& what it is

fuchsia
montbretia
meadowsweet
hedge parsley
purple loosestrife
briars
ferns
rushes
grass

great swathes of wild rhubarb

& later　　　　heather

these words have referents
denote those things that make
a simple system
roadside composition

& raised these stones
out of nothing

& for a reason
(unknown) set them

so & so we look
thusward

out of the pool
they bay
& into night
they slip

ships
into light
determinate

rough hewn
rough dressed
rough mannered

with goods
from York
from Bristol

conduits

tiny bondings

out of nothing
almost air perhaps
these words come
from mind
an imperfect garden

mud on the walls
& our feet
& in our hair

to find
elaborate
sing

out of quiet
complexity

dark it was &
drawing in who
would be there
playing these
streets walked
repeatedly

in sun in rain in-
effable held always

there

out of memory
difficult nearly evaded
which is not

enter the place the sun
people sit a pebble
dressed   water

hope pervades
& is rebuffed

but sun remains

is this
a memory:
water rises

bites a
momentary
drift

hand reaches
dress
billows down

under
a wave
& out

to air
alive
again

long gone it is
this dream a place
to walk in

lost not lost
rebuilt
a mental

city
human &
familiar

river binds
these buildings
gone again

when all are tried
walk out in air crisp
& clear treasure this
morning seen cold as
its absence shrivelled leaves
a new year & here
we go again round
it is cold & dense
bits or air frozen
rare occurrences a shadow
who lived in land
& in town   too

in this place
where nothing grows
it grows

out of soil
frozen a thin
green emerges

& spreads slow
out beyond
such hope

as nurtures us
renewed &
verdant

a pen that was paper
paper that was
that was

a tree that was
words on paper

that were signs
impulses
even connect

paper that was
a tree that was
an impulse

oddly even light
a flame (a
metaphor) shaping
this new thing

briefly flickers a
wake this so
intensely moments
before &

since this is
& cannot be
other a waking
into night

nothing to write tonight
just smile for swirls
round us here & we
are still as ever love
cuts through the rime

& enters entire the world
as we see it so the art
to learn a willow
bare & hoar bends
silently against

the flow of it & stints
nothing but what you need
is in it as it slow
-ly opens   a single bud
furls towards the light

not once   but often
as night say   or memory

flown over   calmly
sweet & low   in sand say

which is   is it not
empty   the time
breaks   open now

& it is night   say warmly

one   over one

these voices   flow

& this is a head

bend it and see

breaking again this day
a flock of images descends
incidental listen
earth heaves & the sky

is witness these attributes
only words give
all that is now
utterly unexpected

ahead the seeds
in this fair field
flowers scatter
growing   through

cold tonight another
ice bites
this unknown city
unseen

as others have
simply passing
no connection
home is

where we go
to be there only
in the centre
something grows

& so

& this is which it was
lost always now
to be in it at one
at once

to go there
& find the place the same
but simplified
same streets
emptied
the past
drained

faces & names
escape a trace
between us hinges
this thing   memory
(layer over layer)
as love is it is
already said

this day replaced
in the stream of things

that are

how to write a star
now that the stars
are classified

great drifts of light
of darkness
nothing
& everything
between

*

slowly
intensely

neither here nor not
neither there nor

light nor darkness

which pass
between

light gathers
impossibly
& fails

the laws are such
& everywhere
they flow

the smallest
flower forms
& everything

that grows
conforms
to process

snow again slightly
is not enough
nothing happens
but the thrill of snow

a withered fuchsia
lit from nowhere
the sense in which
potential strays

& spills again
night assembles
a thing that happens
& grips this page

walk through the great estate
& wonder how rock becomes
property this waterfall a garden
tamed apparently eyes have it so

it is not owned but
borrowed & that badly
& on a false premise
entertained but not proven
we are here
provisional & tenuous

the water moves without us
& within there are torrents
only beyond there are none
the path curves & turns
back & is clear

lost lost lost again
a single yellow crocus
another   a clump
breaking through

this spring morning
as the world unfolds
& rises through frost
& fog these elements

are all that is
that make it flower
& not to freeze
& not be found

if it be so
then there is
the tide of things
turning
(as they might be)
slowly

to meld
into the world
a breath
almost
pushing
simple
streams
of light
away

ice on the windscreen
morning returns
where you are
& where you would be

seen there is no thing
that holds which is
not nothing ever
a car a man

some water a universe
expands from these
particular things
such elements

misremembered
scraping the glass
clear leaving
only again

it melts it flows
is not as it was
vision draws out
the necessary end

where there is nothing
buds show through
& all returns
to flux:

not spring
but its semblance
not winter
but its fading

grass bent &
trees reluctant
a sudden southerly
winds its way

these easy patterns

listen
& you can see
things change

a process
only
everything
flowing

old metal wheel-rim in a ditch
rusted & splendid & trapped
in scutch as evidence
of habitation

once here or near a house
long gone only these traces
bring us near a life sustained
against occurrences
at the edge of all that is
curved resilient & worn

spinning: engine off
& rolling smoothly
freewheel under
mottled light

bend & slow
another climbs
to where we've been
just now & left

to this degree
summer fades
lingers warm
& somewhat free

tonight there are no words
& so we speak this silence

rain moving a distant train
the stars in rare trajectory

where all sounds sweet
we hang above
traffic

voices nothing internal
but gentle
stilled now

a place remembered as
never known
awaiting

rain enters night
which is all
here so

& matters meekly
the wind asseverates
to cross the waiting green

time is spent between
here and the world's sweet
lulling   sounds disturb

the fabric settle down now
& enter sleep

that there is
what is
& is enough

flows
over   the weir
under   the bridge

& goes
gives way
the same river
same water
same place

these new leaves open
to possibility spring
it must be
when all is loss

recovered visibility
erased & clear
light folds round
& eases through

turn in the sun
& wonder what it is
that turns

& lives here long
under the sign
of turning

a melody strays
across the day
no song

but sun's circuit
we turn in it
& turn

nothing is made but is
perception evaded
life moves
& age holds all

as if it could envision
something beside
this river teemed
a sound recognised

as things go through
this earth &
warm it rises
warm it grows

who that comes
here now
that keeps
words away

who that moves
aware as when
a flowering
these words are

as music moves
that which comes
keeping as when
these words end

sleep slips by
as it may

when it is lived
as it is

everything ends this
road goes no further
& we have not arrived

where the road goes
& nothing more
but the wending

a snatch of music
heard beyond
the ear's range

it makes no sense a future
walk beyond the bounds
& see the things you wanted
drifting who was & was not
sleeping under pressure
intense snatches heard the ear's
range displayed silent &
sweet as night enclosed these
trees feel it it makes no matter
along this line weaving
something unfinished yet

slowly build & slowly
navigate roots lie
in this effort

to rise & go
whichever way
it flows not much

a line of trade a way
out of the world
before great waves

fill the air & ring
all that is this
& is no more

come near
this glimpse
of all we need

nothing here
stand in the garden
say life is so

& mean it strange
to be here again
awake in beauty

wind
sea
sky

simple
elements

a day
a journey
on arrival

all these
are things
that are

spaces
illuminate

the great dish
drifts
& falls

an apogee
reached

decline
follows

walk through dunes
the wind abates &
undulates beneath your
feet & rise above the blue
the sand yields little
to reason grass binds
lightly pass between

attending these words
the birds attends
cat on the wall
morning unfolds
long & unmolested

events   moments
all are attended
clear   bird   cat
light after rain
after the night

say a moment's
inattention costs
everything slips away
the day extends
beyond these things

& so end here
where land &
water are
indistinguishable

air also edge
& myriad things
colour the light
alive with what

is essence extends
these few demands
& so
begin

recession of planes:
mountains lit from within
it seems each one its own
space real & yet not
sure now land arrives

across the glen
trees   rock   mist
rain between which
light moves (it doesn't)
walk the land & see

earth water fire & air

but mostly water

are we there yet?

we're here now